LOVE IS...

WALKING
HAND-IN-HAND

BY
CHARLES
M.
SCHULZ

First paperback edition 1971
Revised, expanded paperback edition 1983
Reprint of revised, expanded paperback edition 1990

Based on "Love is Walking Hand in Hand"
by Charles M. Schulz

Published by Determined Productions, Inc.
Box 2150, San Francisco, CA 94126
Printed in Hong Kong

ISBN 0-915696-80-0
Library of Congress Catalog Card No. 79-63490

The first edition of LOVE IS WALKING HAND-IN-HAND, written and illustrated by world-famous cartoonist Charles M. Schulz, appeared in 1965.

This little volume followed the lead of an earlier Schulz triumph, HAPPINESS IS A WARM PUPPY, and became an immediate success.

Now LOVE IS WALKING HAND-IN-HAND is back in a new and enlarged version. This revised edition, all in color, contains three times as many pages, full of new Schulz drawings and sentiments.

Snoopy and the entire PEANUTS®gang are on hand again — and that means a whole lot of fun as well as a whole lot of LOVE!

Don't forget to ask for the new and enlarged version of HAPPINESS IS A WARM PUPPY, too.

Love is
having
a special
song.

Love is
accepting
a person
for what
he is.

Love is sharing your popcorn.

Love is
getting someone
a glass of water
in the middle
of the night.

Love is
a valentine
with lace
all around
the edges.

Love is looking out for your friends.

Love is
a phone call.

Love is
a helping
hand.

Love is
trust.

Love is being nominated neighborhood dog of the year.

Love is
eating out with
your whole
family.

Love is rooting together for your team.

Love is
wanting
to make
someone
smile.

Love is
listening
without
interrupting.

Love is
being polite
to people.

Love is
helping your
team to win.

Love is
visiting
a sick friend.

Love is
watching
someone else's
boring show
on T.V.

Love is
sitting
all the way
through
a recital.

Love is
believing
in someone.

Love is
not littering.

Love is
helping someone
through his
battles.

Love is
hoping that
she hasn't
forgotten
you.

Love is
walking
in the rain
together.

Love is making fudge together.

Love is
flowers from
your favorite
person.

Love is being tolerant.

Love is
meeting someone
by the pencil
sharpener.

Love is
letting your
house guest
have your
room.

Love is
waking
someone up
from a bad
dream.

Love is
making plans
together.

Love is
wondering
what he's doing
right now this
very moment.

Love is
being
a good
loser.

Love is
buying somebody
a present
with your
own money.

Love is
passing notes
back and forth
in school.

Love is
being
hospitable.

Love is
letting him win
even though you
know you could
slaughter
him.

Love is
being happy
just knowing
that she's happy...
but that
isn't so easy.

Love is
dressing up
for someone.

Love is
a push
in the right
direction.

Love is
not nagging.

Love is
being faithful
to the very
end.

Love is
when your friends
ask to give you
a testimonial
dinner.

Love is
tickling.

Love is
an invitation
to lunch.

Love is
allowing someone
to sleep late.

Love is
committing
yourself
in writing.

Love is
hating to say
goodbye.

Love is
mussing up
someone's
hair.

Love is
loaning your
best comic
magazines.

Love is
walking
hand-in-hand.

Love is
helping your
sister with her
homework.

Love is
a letter
on pink
stationery.

Love is
being a good
watch dog.

Love is
wishing you had
nerve enough
to go over
and talk with
that little girl
with the
red hair.

Love is
being patient
with your
little brother.

Love is
close
dancing.

Love is
standing in a
doorway just to see
her if she comes
walking by.

Love is
a flag.

Love is
a goodnight
kiss.

Love is
a smile
even when
he keeps you
waiting.

Love is
the whole
world.